Emil Schulthess / ETERNAL LANDSCAPE

Emil Schulthess

ETERNAL

LANDSCAPE

Utah · Arizona · Colorado · New Mexico

Text by Sigmund Widmer

Alfred A. Knopf New York 1988

THIS IS A BORZOI BOOK
PUBLISHED BY ALFRED A. KNOPF, INC.

 Published in the United States by Alfred A. Knopf, Inc., New York, and simultaneously in Canada by Random House of Canada Limited, Toronto. Distributed by Random House, Inc., New York. First published in Switzerland by Meridian Press, CH-8127 Forch/Zurich, in 1987.

Photographs and design: Emil Schulthess
Text: Dr. Sigmund Widmer
Translation: Anthony J. Lloyd

Library of Congress Cataloging in Publication Data
Schulthess, Emil.
Eternal Landscape.
English version of: Millions of years ago
(a trilingual ed.). © 1987.
1. Southwest, New—Description and travel—1981—. 2. Southwest, New—Description and travel—1981—Views. 3. National parks and reserves—Southwest, New. 4. National parks and reserves—Southwest, New—Pictorial works.
5. Photography—Southwest, New—Landscapes.
I. Widmer, Sigmund II. Title.
F787.S38 1988 917.9'0022'2 88-6767
ISBN 0-394-57144-4

Manufactured in Switzerland
First American Edition

Contents

Preface

Can we date the prehistoric era? Was it three million years ago, when man first appeared? Or 140 million years ago, when archosauria inhabited the continents? Or perhaps 350 million years ago, when fish ventured onto dry land? Or even earlier, when the land "rose" out of the sea?

In the southwest United States is to be found one of the best vantage points for a look back into the multi-million-year history of our planet. Here a creative hand working in alternating periods of warmth and cold fashioned earth and sky, land and water, into a monument of gigantic temporal and spatial dimensions—of a vastness beyond the scope of the layman's imagination and, for the scientist, allowing no more than speculative assumptions that are constantly called into question. Our dimensional conceptions are too modest to allow us to visualize and quantify the origins and evolution of life on this earth. The whole dispute between creationism and Darwinism pales into insignificance if we consider the four billion years of the earth's history as a geological clock scaled down to a twenty-four-hour earth day: in that scenario, man only appeared in the last minute.

A look through the window of this primeval landscape can do no more than throw the faintest glimmer of light on what happened before man arrived on the scene. We are obliged to recognize that we are advancing only gradually away from our ignorance towards certain knowledge. The geological panorama displayed in this volume testifies to a creative diversity which even the 20th century can only regard with wonderment. Whose imagination can fail to be moved by the colossal, soaring rock formations, the magic temples and cathedrals, the towers and pinnacles, skyscrapers and gothic castles—inhabited and surrounded by the petrified gods of the earliest inhabitants, whose rich mythology paid homage to the "weeping cliff" and to the spot where "the rainbow sleeps."

How impressive indeed are those ancient rock structures generated by the interacting forces of sun and wind, water and stone, which tell us something of the earliest days of the earth's existence. And in the midst of all this, recalling the "third day" on which the earth was made verdant, are trees and plants bearing witness to the mystery of primeval life: the 100 million-year-old owl gnat set in amber and the petrified tracks of dinosaurs in mud. Everywhere we come upon evidence of the creative process, filling us with awe and admonishing us to temper the unbridled hubris which typifies the modern age.

That is the quiet message contained in this book, calling us to reflect as we peruse the oldest history-book on planet earth and opening our eyes to the beauty of the world around us: "Mysterious all—yet all is good, all fair as at the birth of light!"

Bruno Mariacher

Eternal Landscape

The southwestern United States is a sparsely populated area with very little industry. This absence of human activity is specially striking along the upper reaches of the Colorado River and in parts of the states of Arizona, Utah and New Mexico. Surprisingly early—at the beginning of the present century—the Federal Government declared that certain regions of outstanding scenic interest were to be national monuments under permanent protection. Thus there came into being the thirty-eight National Parks, some of which are described in pictures and words in this volume.

What have these examples of the monumental workings of nature in common with one another? They are all located in an arid climate where the layer of humus generally found in temperate zones is almost entirely absent; moreover, most of the volatile sand formations usually lying beneath the humus have been swept away by desert winds. A geologist searching for such exposure would need to be very patient if he kept to the temperate zones with their mantle of woods, meadows, and fields interspersed with human settlements. The American southwest, by contrast, offers something like a single, unified exposure enabling even the layman with an interest in geology to gain a direct insight into the nature of the rock structures. The geological ages are presented with almost unparalleled clarity. What could be more natural, therefore, than to wander—with the geologist's hammer held at least symbolically in one's hand—through these enthralling regions?

Their extraordinary fascination is of course due to other characteristics as well. First, there are the magnificent colorings. The high mineral content of many strata often lends the rock a range of colors extending from bright white through yellow, ochre, orange, light red, brown, purple, violet, green, and grey to dark blue and even black. It was not by chance that the mighty natural arch on a fjord off Lake Powell was given the name of "Rainbow Bridge."

This superb variety of color is accompanied in places by a simply unbelievable wealth of forms. In Bryce Canyon, Monument Valley, Arches National Park, and elsewhere the eye is astounded by unusual rock formations. The bizarre towers seem to mock the law of gravity, making it hard at first to believe that they actually owe their origin to a creative caprice of nature rather than to the hand of man.

These characteristics are further enhanced by the extreme dryness of the climate. Day after day the sun conjures up the most multifarious color effects in the rocky landscape, those occurring when the sun is low naturally being the most spectacular. The almost permanently clear air renders shapes and light effects unrealistically distinct. Nor should we forget among this catalogue of wonders the colors to be seen in winter. Parts of these National Parks lie above 6,000 feet, areas in which the white of winter snow forms an enchanting contrast to the red or violet of the rocks. And since it is also largely without vegetation and even to some extent sterile, this terrain tends to give visitors the feeling of having left the earth and strayed to the moon or another planet.

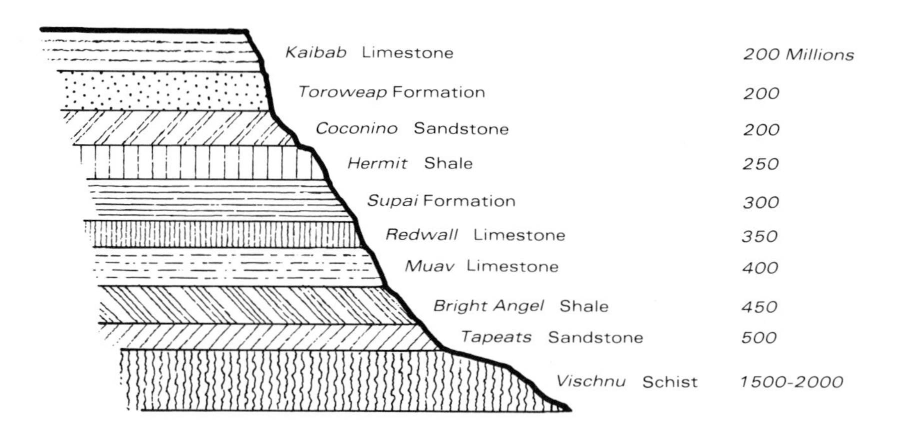

Visitors often feel they should learn more about those adventurous souls who first intruded into this inhospitable region. Early Stone Age settlers were eventually obliged to make way for the different tribes generally referred to as American Indians. The sixteenth-century invasion by Spanish adventurers, mainly in the south, was followed in the eighteenth century by the arrival of pioneers of English origin who advanced westwards as far as the Colorado Plateau. The Mormons who were bold enough to settle here around the middle of the nineteenth-century, chiefly in the state of Utah, constructed impressive irrigation systems. Then, in the second half of the century, came the first scientifically minded explorers, who combined their love of adventure with a modern interest in more serious matters. Finally, our own century brought the age of tourism and with it a desire for conservation.

The most interesting aspect of the southwestern nature reserves, however, is probably their geology. Looking from the South Rim of the Grand Canyon towards the northerly cliff-face opposite, which drops in stages through almost 6,000 feet, we are presented with an unequalled panorama of the earth's early history. "In the course of a few million years, water, wind, cold and heat have created a plateau landscape with rock strata up to four billion years old, conveying some idea of the geological time dimension." (Jörg Negendank *Geologie*, München 1981, p. 14). Here indeed we find, tidily ordered in horizontal stages, rock varieties reflecting a large part of the earth's history. These strata are represented in the diagram at top left. It should be noted, however, that

ZION CANYON

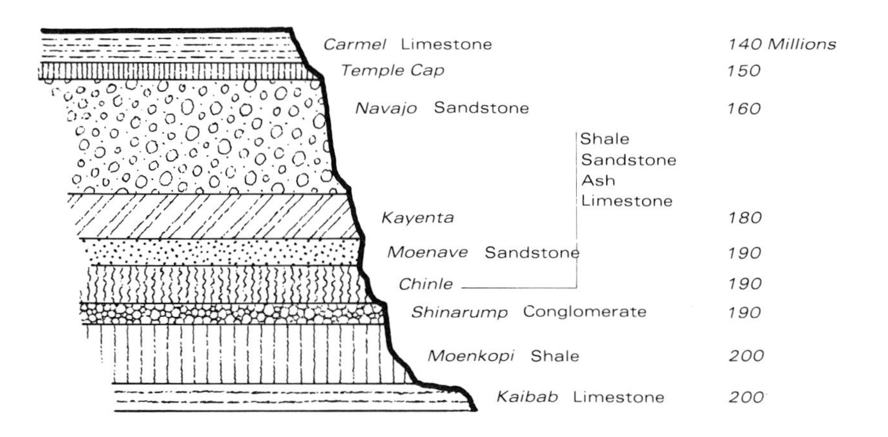

expert opinion differs widely about the periods of time involved. To be on the safe side, therefore, the figures given are averages representing the "present state of uncertain knowledge."

Erosion, it should be remembered, has wiped out quite a number of more recent rock strata above the Kaibab limestone. But in Zion Canyon these sediments have been preserved. In other words, the lowest stratum in Zion Canyon (top right) could in theory be laid on top of the uppermost stratum of the Grand Canyon.

Mention has been made of land almost devoid of vegetation, but this needs some qualification. Strictly, the description applies only to zones with an annual rainfall of less than 8 inches. Higher regions, beginning with the north side of the Grand Canyon (about 7,500 feet) but including the northern parts of Bryce and Zion, are covered in thin woodland including the Ponderosa pine, Douglas fir, silver fir, and numerous bushes such as the sage. Particularly enchanting are the river oases of varying sizes, some artificially enlarged. Even in dry regions—at least in spring and late summer—herbs and grasses spring up vigorously to form patches of succulent green and bloom-laden splendor. Cacti flourish where the land is extremely arid. In intermediate zones, stunted oaks and junipers predominate.

More or less the same applies to the fauna, which accommodates itself to the plant life. A small number of pumas and mountain lions still live in the forests, but a more frequent resident is the mule deer. The coyote is common and among the many species of birds the golden eagle is king.

Various types of squirrel are present in large numbers, as are those lizards indigenous to dry regions.

Despite their variety, the landscapes illustrated on the following pages form a single whole. They are, after all, unusual examples of our earth's surface. Anyone who studies the geology of these regions looks back upon the history of our planet—a view encompassing hundreds of millions of years.

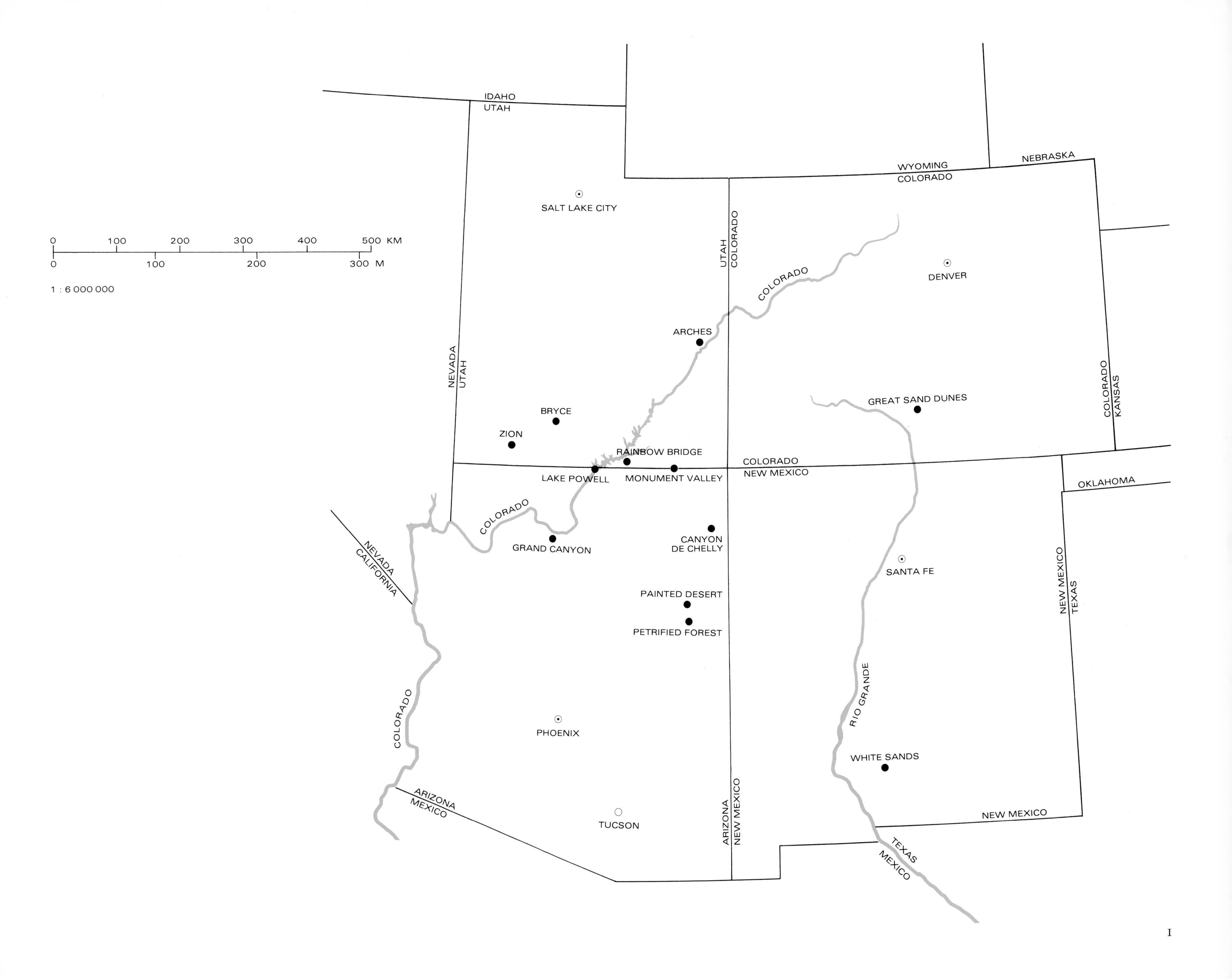
IDAHO
UTAH
WYOMING
COLORADO
NEBRASKA
SALT LAKE CITY
0 100 200 300 400 500 KM
0 100 200 300 M
1 : 6 000 000
UTAH
COLORADO
COLORADO
DENVER
ARCHES
NEVADA
UTAH
COLORADO
KANSAS
GREAT SAND DUNES
BRYCE
ZION
RAINBOW BRIDGE
COLORADO
NEW MEXICO
LAKE POWELL
MONUMENT VALLEY
OKLAHOMA
COLORADO
GRAND CANYON
CANYON
DE CHELLY
NEVADA
CALIFORNIA
SANTA FE
NEW MEXICO
TEXAS
PAINTED DESERT
PETRIFIED FOREST
RIO GRANDE
COLORADO
PHOENIX
WHITE SANDS
ARIZONA
MEXICO
TUCSON
ARIZONA
NEW MEXICO
NEW MEXICO
TEXAS
MEXICO

Zion

Geologically, Zion National Park belongs to the Colorado region. In the course of several million years the Virgin River ate its way through a variety of rock strata. The uppermost stratum of Carmel limestone lies roughly 1,800 to 2,500 feet above the lowest one composed of Kaibab limestone, which as already mentioned forms the top stratum of the Grand Canyon. The rock most severely worn away is Navajo sandstone. These quartz sand strata, deposited in swamps, alluvial plains, and deserts (in the latter case by the wind), solidified into sandstone. Navajo sandstone contains numerous oxides of iron and manganese which give delightful colorings to the often vertical canyon walls (2). The lowest formations are probably some two hundred thirty million years old. The geology of the Zion region was also affected in the very recent past by volcanic activity, providing a sharp contrast. In the central area of the park, in particular, younger basalt overlies the old sedimentary rock.

Although a semi-desert climate prevails, substantial differences occur according to altitude. The higher and more northerly areas of the park are rainier and cooler with over 20 inches of precipitation a year. In January, temperatures can sink to −77° F. In the southern parts, annual precipitation amounts to about 14 inches. While average temperatures in July reach approximately 82°, the thermometer can rise to over 113°.

Plant growth is appropriately desert-like. The high plateaux are covered with sparse woodland consisting largely of Ponderosa pine (Pinus ponderosa) (1). Along the Virgin River,

I

2

3

which travels 144 miles on its way through Zion Park and falls roughly 3,870 feet, small river oases are found, some of them artificial, planted by early inhabitants. Otherwise the vegetation is extremely modest (3, 4). Spring is the time when it is at its most attractive. The fauna, too, is correspondingly limited in variety. An occasional mule deer shows itself and mountain lions inhabit the hinterland, shunning man. Foxes and raccoons are also found, of course, preying in their turn on smaller wildlife. The most common animal of all is said to be the coyote, which will eat anything. Zion Canyon boasts a very wide variety of birds, of which the golden eagle is the most splendid example.

The prehistoric Anasazi were the first human inhabitants whose presence can be demonstrated for certain. They vanished for some unknown reason around the thirteenth century, but left behind them a pueblo (village) and rock drawings. They were followed in the area by the Paiute Indians, of whom some 700 still live in Utah today. The first white men to venture into the Virgin gorge were Mormons, who lived peacefully with the Indians and gave its present name to this monumental miracle of nature: alluding to Jerusalem's Mount Zion, the symbolic refuge of the Old Testament, they called the almost inaccessible valley a "place of quiet and safety."

Bryce Canyon

Bryce Canyon, unlike Zion National Park, is not in fact a canyon or gorge in the proper sense of those terms, a watercourse and its tributaries having eroded a kind of amphitheatre out of the soft limestone (5, 6). The Paiute Indians named the valley basin appositely "Red rocks standing like men in a bowl-shaped ravine." Gnawed at by the water, the plateau has retained to this day the name originally given it by the Paiutes: Paunsaugunt or Land of the Beavers. The plateau's edge recedes by an average of an inch a year.

This so-called Wasatchian rock formation which yields so willingly to the action of water is a relatively young, argillaceous limestone stratum 490 to 530 feet thick. Also known as Pink Cliffs, it came into being about sixty-five million years ago, when river-borne mud and silt were deposited in a large fresh-water lake. Later, a good seventeen million years ago, the gorge was raised some 9,000 feet and the sedimentary mantle disintegrated into gigantic slabs or blocks. One of these slabs is the Paunsaugunt Plateau. Exposed to the elements, the once almost horizontal limestone strata have been transformed into weird towers and ledges of rock (7).

The effects of erosion differ greatly with the varying firmness of the Wasatchian formation, the softer portions wearing down more rapidly than the more resistant ones. This process has resulted in the most extraordinary profiles in both vertical and horizontal directions (8), with harder formations left standing like columns. Not infrequently, window-like holes form in narrow fins of rock resembling walls. Weather-resistant strata make huge caps on top of breathtakingly thin

4

towers (9). The whole structure is further enriched by magnificent coloring where iron and manganese inject reds, blues, violets, and even blackish-blues into the original whites and light yellows of the Wasatchian limestone. Looking out onto this sublime creation of nature from one of the prominent and easily accessible vantage points at sunrise or sunset, one can scarcely help being overwhelmed by a feeling of gratitude.

Lake Powell / Rainbow Bridge

Today the Colorado River is dammed at several points on its long journey out of the mountains just west of Denver down to the Gulf of California. Easily the largest of these artificial lakes is Lake Powell, named after John Wesley Powell (1834–1902), an American geologist and ethnologist who, while exploring in 1869, became the first man to negotiate the Grand Canyon by boat, and who also made a name for himself through his knowledge of Indian languages. Without counting its almost innumerable lateral arms, Lake Powell with its many contortions extends some 125 miles as far as the town of Page. As figure 11 shows (taken near Page), the deep blue water of this reservoir offers a gloriously colorful contrast to the surrounding yellowish-brown plateau almost entirely bereft of vegetation.

An exceptionally interesting experience is the five-mile boat trip from the dam to Rainbow Bridge, particularly the final stretch giving access to Bridge Creek (12, 13, 14)—previously more or less dry—and to within a comfortable 1,300 feet of an astonishing marvel of nature. Rainbow Bridge is the largest known natural arch in the world (16). Most visitors, even if already familiar with this natural "structure" from photographs, are amazed by the sight confronting them. Reaching up to a height of 290 feet, the sandstone bridge is equivalent in size to a skyscraper of almost thirty stories. At its highest point the arch has a diameter of 43 feet. The impression is further enhanced by the curious salmon-pink coloring, which in the evening light in particular displays a multitude of nuances fully justifying the name given to this mighty structure. Rocky domes

10

15

scoured smooth by sandstorms over many thousands of years lend the landscape a mysterious, unreal character. In the southeast, blue Mount Navajo (15) rises 9,500 feet out of the bare plain.

The experts are more or less agreed as to the origins of this strange phenomenon. The base of the arch consists of hard Kayenta rock overlaid with a substantial stratum of Navajo sandstone about 900 feet thick. The Colorado Plateau was raised approximately sixty million years ago, after which the present system of watercourses formed. As elsewhere, the waters flowing into the Colorado from Mount Navajo worked on the limestone mountains in their path. Initially the Bridge River as it then was meandered its way around the obstacle and the meander may conceivably have approached very closely to the water flowing further up and eroded the limestone face from two sides. In this way the water eventually sought and found a more direct course. Thus, as millennia passed by, softer portions dissolved while a harder, arch-shaped section resisted and stands to this day.

In 1909, W. B. Douglass and Byron Cummings worked their way through this impassable region after hearing from Paiute Indians that a great stone arch stood not far from Mount Navajo. News of the discovery spread quickly. By 1910 a small thirty-acre area around Rainbow Bridge had been declared a National Park. It will long continue to attract an admiring public to this desert region, where summer temperatures can be very high despite the altitude of 3,350 feet above sea level.

Arches

Directly to the north of the town of Moab, which takes its name from Israel's Old Testament neighbor, lies Arches National Park, bounded on its southern side by the upper reaches of the Colorado. As the name suggests, this area close to the Colorado state border is distinguished by an unusually large number of stone arches (17, 19), together with a huge variety of rock formations [Park Avenue (18), Garden of Eden (20)]. The park is of considerable size, extending over more than 19 miles in a north-south direction. The arches are spread around here and there in bigger and smaller groups, over two hundred of them having a width of opening of at least 3 feet. Visiting all these unusual rock structures is of course a very time-consuming affair.

Geologists assume that a stratum of salt was deposited here about three hundred million years ago as sea water evaporated. Later, so the theory goes, further layers of mud and sand were left on top, partly by lakes and partly through the action of desert winds. In the course of many millions of years, these strata grew to a thickness of some 4,000 feet. Under the enormous weight the bed of salt subsided, producing a variety of clefts and folds of which the best known is the Moab Fault north of Moab. Whenever the climate was wet, water entered these clefts and dissolved the limestone. In cooler periods, ice formation accelerated the erosion process. In the more delicate formations of the Entsada sandstone and in the Navajo sandstone, the once firmly cohesive horizontal strata were reduced to ever narrower, wall-like fins (18). These finally became so thin that only the most resistant portions remained. The result was the multitude of towers standing for the most part in

groups but occasionally alone (17, 18, 19). Especially spectacular are those structures where no more than wafer-thin arches remain, like mighty gates defying the laws of gravity, like "Delicate Arch" (17) with a height of about 75 feet and the "Landscape Arch" (19) which reaches a span of 300 feet.

As in Bryce Canyon, the varying consistency of the strata has produced absurd formations which the desert winds have worn smooth and round, making a striking spectacle for the human eye (20). No wonder some of the earliest travellers thought these astonishing structures were the work not of nature but of man, like the megaliths of Stonehenge in England.

One of the first settlers in this desolate country was John Wesley Wolfe, a Civil War veteran who arrived in 1888 and made a living by breeding cattle. Wolfe Ranch still stands today, conveying to the visitor a powerful image of the hard life of the pioneer.

Grand Canyon

The Grand Canyon is easily the best known natural wonder among the regions discussed in this book, and it is likely to have been inhabited the longest. In its caves have been found rock drawings and other traces of Stone Age cultures going back several thousand years. It was in 1540 that the first white men, Spanish adventurers, reached the South Rim (21) and experienced the breathtaking view of one of the world's most gigantic and impressive gorges (22). The Grand River, as the Colorado was still called at that time, was not properly explored in the modern sense until about 1870, by Major John Wesley Powell. The first permanent inhabitants of the Industrial Age were miners in search of copper and other minerals, who on their departure left behind them mules which ran wild. The canyon has been a tourist attraction since about the beginning of the present century. The first deluxe hotel, the El Tovar, opened in 1905, and the valley was declared a National Park in 1919. Today the Grand Canyon enjoys great popularity, although the North Rim is less overrun than the fully accessible South Rim.

In geological terms the Grand Canyon differs fundamentally from all the regions described so far. The Colorado River has bored much deeper into the earth's crust (23) and we can therefore look back at much older rock strata, the lowest of which are probably some two billion years old. The chronological sequence of the strata is illustrated on page x. Originally the Colorado Plateau was drained in a southeasterly direction, but the slope shifted about 6,000 feet during the great tectonic elevation and after that the water flowed away towards the southwest. Roughly seventeen

million years ago, the original Colorado began to work on strata which have since vanished almost completely, but are still visible in Bryce Canyon (see p. 12, 17). The most attractive is the six hundred seventy-foot stratum of red limestone in the middle of the wall (24), with overhanging crags. It probably came into existence some three hundred twenty-five million years ago, when marine organisms were deposited; the red tone is due to iron oxides from the strata above.

Most appealing of all, however, is the complete picture created by the two walls. There can hardly be another site in the world where rock strata dating back a billion years are juxtaposed in such a way that even the layman can easily appreciate the relation borne by one to another.

Monument Valley

Travelling further east from the Grand Canyon, we pass through Kayenta and after about 170 miles arrive at Monument Valley. This is perhaps one of America's most famous regions, the curiously romantic combination of desert and bizarre rock formations having been used for half a century as a backdrop for countless films, television programs, and advertisements. John Ford was one of the first to recognize its special charm—it was here that in 1938 he shot "Stagecoach", and, in 1946, "My Darling Clementine." Modern dream factories and the profit-conscious publicity industry soon learned the trick of turning the fascination of this landscape into money.

The most striking feature of this dramatic scenery is probably the bold contrast between the severely horizontal lines of a seemingly endless, broad plateau (lying some 5,500 feet above sea level) and individual bodies of rock towering up in a sheer craze of verticality. So idiosyncratic is the effect that these have been given their own names: in figure 28, left of center, "West Mitten Butte", right of center, "East Mitten Butte", far right, "Merrick Butte"; in figure 29, far right, "Totem Pole."

What were the origins of so remarkable a landscape? Geologists tell us that the horizontal strata were formed over two million years ago. They belonged to the Cutler Formation (De Chelly sandstone, Organ Rock tongue, Hoskinnonni tongue) dating from the Permian Period, and were later overlaid with harder sediments from the Rocky Mountains. These are Shinarump conglomerates, Moenconi and Chinle Formations, all dating from the Triassic Period. Volcanic interstratification can also be observed, these younger strata being harder and more resistant to

29

30

erosion. While the Grand Canyon, for example, is a single valley cut out of the sedimentary strata, we are confronted here with a completely different process, almost the whole of a plateau having been removed. Solitary rock structures which resisted erosion soar towards the sky, some resembling fingers, some like fantastic castles. Quite a number reach up to a height of about a thousand feet. While some rise straight out of the plain, others have the semblance of a base which makes them easier to climb.

The pictures (29–33) taken by Emil Schulthess in the fall of 1983 have a special rarity value, because his visit coincided with a period of unusually damp weather. As a result the air is not shown as it normally appears, clear and dry; instead, the buttes and fingers are veiled in strange mists such as occur here only very infrequently (31).

It should be mentioned that Monument Valley is situated in the huge Navajo Reservation covering sixteen million acres or 25,000 square miles and containing scattered settlements with a total of 160,000 Navajos. People often refer to the "Navajo Nation," which has its own capital at Window Rock, Arizona. This emphasis on independence and self-administration symbolizes a desire of today's American people to make amends to the Navajos, who were cruelly decimated in the second half of the nineteenth century. Monument Valley Tribal Park was one of the first (1958) designed to give the Indians permanent peace and material security.

Great Sand Dunes

Along its upper reaches around Alamosa, the Rio Grande crosses a flat plateau, the San Luis Valley (roughly 7,000 feet). Geologically a tectonic fault trough, this exceedingly arid valley situated at a considerable altitude is shielded to the west by the San Juan Mountains and to the north and east by the Sangre de Cristo Mountains. A most unusual tract of dune country, which formed at the foot of this second mountain range over a period of thousands of years, was declared a National Monument in 1932 (40).

Experts differ as to how such an isolated dune region could have come into being, although they do agree that there must have been some interaction between mountains, valleys, and climate. The dunes probably appeared at the end of the last Ice Age, in other words some 10,000 years ago, when melted snow and ice from the surrounding mountains carried sand, gravel, and mud down into the valley. Most important, the Rio Grande must have brought quantities of fine-grained materials down out of the San Juan Mountains.

The unusual mountain formations all around channel the winds—blowing mainly from the southwest—in so-called wind traps. As a result, sand that all the while became increasingly fine was blown here and there in a more or less closed circuit over thousands of years, trapped inside the San Luis Valley. Partly at rest, partly on the move, the dunes cover an area of 155 square miles. They are certainly the highest ones in America, some of their summits reaching above 600 feet (38). Unlike White Sands, the sand here is a rusty-brown color sometimes shading into grey and ochre (37).

Winter in particular sets these vivid colors off most attractively against the snowy white of the Sangre de Cristo Mountains. Over the Great Sand Dunes, too, the air is almost always dry and produces astonishing color effects, especially when the sunlight falls at an angle.

Spectacularly beautiful the landscape may be, but let it never be forgotten that walks of any length through the dunes can be dangerous. It is an easy matter to misjudge distances and get lost. In summer, the sand becomes so hot that shoes are indispensable. During thunderstorms, the ridges of the dunes become electrically charged and attract lightning. Water, moreover, is non-existent. Medano Creek, on the eastern edge of the dunes, seeps away after a few miles. Water has to be carried as a valued ration.

Folsom Man, the earliest form of homo sapiens to hunt in this region, must have witnessed the emergence of the Great Sand Dunes. The pueblo peoples settled on the periphery of the dunes sometime after the beginning of the Christian era. It was probably in 1694 that the first Spaniards arrived in this inhospitable area on the very edge of Spanish-controlled territory. The first reports of English-speaking settlers date from about 1807, but not until around 1920 did word spread about the existence of these mighty dunes, attracting the first tourists to the San Luis Valley.

Canyon de Chelly

The name de Chelly is not, as one might suppose, derived from an aristocratic Frenchman's surname. The word has its origin in the language of the Navajo Indians: "Tsegi" means valley of rock. The Spanish pronunciation "day skay-yee" was again transformed in English and according to the park rangers the name is now pronounced "d'shay."

We now return from our geological detour into the southern Rocky Mountains and the source of the Rio Grande to the Colorado Plateau. Canyon de Chelly lies far to the east, near the Four Corners where the four states of Arizona, New Mexico, Colorado, and Utah come together. Canyon de Chelly is situated in a remote, thinly populated region at the southeast foot of the Chuska Mountains. Theoretically the valley drains through the Chinle Wash into the Colorado.

The ancient Rio de Chelly began its patient work seventeen million years ago, boring its way with many meanders into vast sedimentary strata now some two hundred million years old. The eye is caught immediately by the sheer sandstone walls—in some parts quite smooth, in others fashioned into the most bizarre shapes (41–45)—which confine a narrow, flat-bottomed valley on both sides (47). Particularly impressive are the dilapidated Indian dwellings nestling at a vertiginous height, as though stuck onto narrow ledges of rock (41, 42). The isolated sandstone towers such as Spider Rock (46), soaring up vertically to over 760 feet, are a strikingly attractive feature.

In periods with more rainfall the valley evidently offered an adequate livelihood. The remains of several hundred Indian settlements have been found, the majority dating from between 300 and

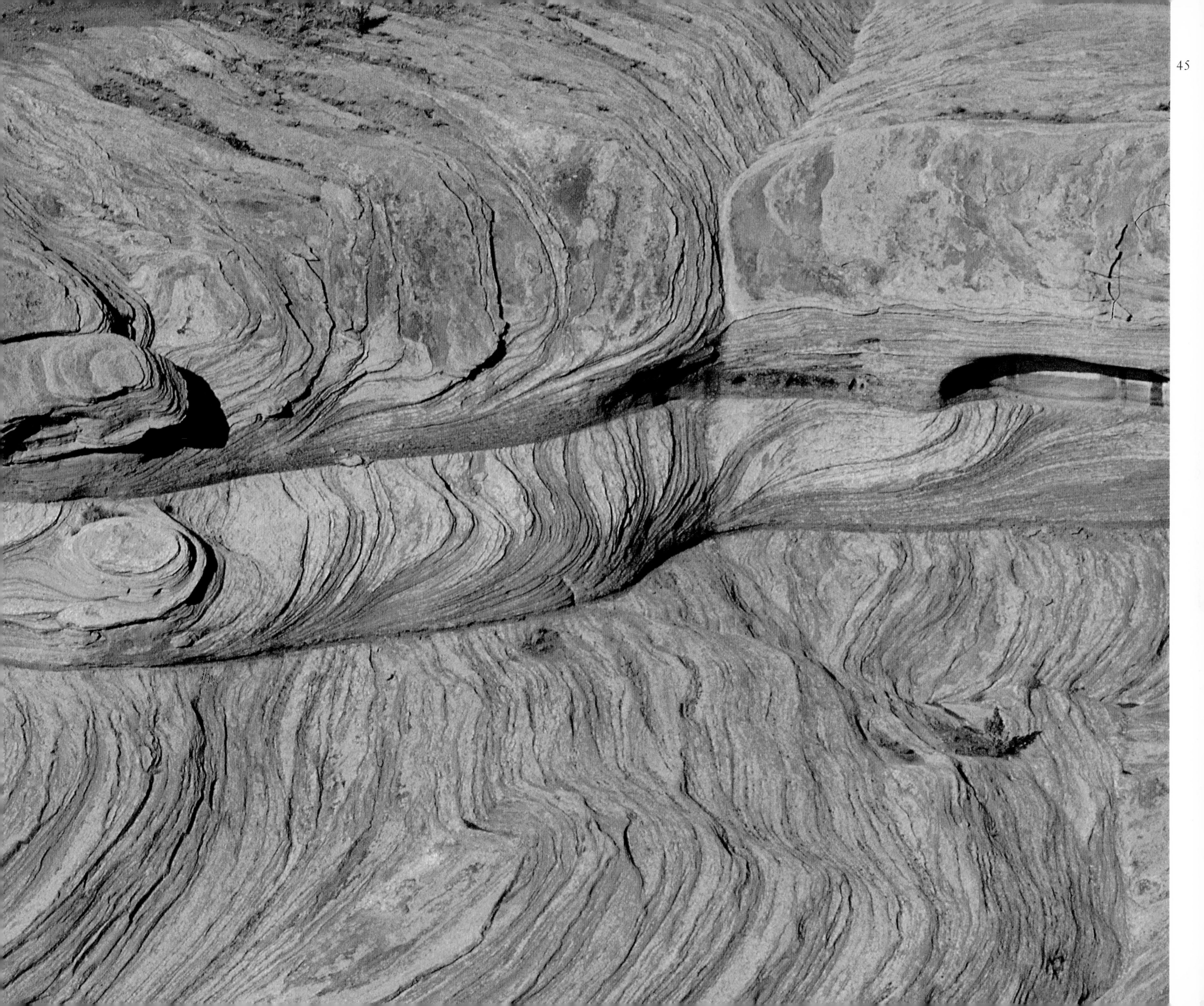

1300 A.D. The houses referred to above were inhabited by Anasazi Indians, who cultivated the river oases (44). The Anasazi are also known as basketmakers; for centuries they were unacquainted with the potter's craft and made most of their essential utensils of wickerwork (using, for example, the leaves of the yucca plant). Their dwellings are assumed to have been constructed between 1100 and 1300, and the choice of location suggests that the inhabitants felt severely threatened by enemies. At any rate, whoever built them vanished around 1300, possibly emigrating and becoming integrated with the pueblo peoples. From time to time thereafter, the de Chelly region was inhabited by the Hopi Indians. Then, around 1700, the area became the heartland of the bellicose and widely distributed Navajo Indians, related to the Apaches. The Navajos had the misfortune to be caught up not only in the northward expansion of the Spaniards but also in the Americans' drive towards the west. Despite resisting the white invasion stubbornly they were forced to capitulate, their final defeat occurring in 1864 when General J. H. Carleton took the de Chelly canyon. Initially forced into humiliating captivity, the Navajos were allowed to return to their homeland in 1868 and now own a spacious reservation. About a hundred Navajos spend the summer in the de Chelly canyon and visitors are obviously under an obligation to respect the rights of the inhabitants. Photographs, for example, may be taken only with the permission of the subjects.

geologists call the Chinle Formation. That was followed by a further phase during which deposits continued to build up, until a time about seventy million years ago, parts of this sedimentary stratum of clayey limestone growing to a thickness of 3,000 feet. During the Tertiary Period of the Cenozoic Era—beginning some sixty-five million years ago—this stratum started to rise, eventually attaining 6,000 feet. This upward movement was more pronounced in the east, where once again lakes were formed. Geologists call this body of water formerly covering the actual area of Painted Desert, Lake Bidahochi. Roughly ten million years ago the rivers started to move in their present westerly direction, the climate became drier, and the lakes disappeared. Four million years ago volcanic eruptions covered the lake basins with lava and ash. The watercourses, some of which are still at work today, ate into this series of strata while weathering brought about further erosion, often penetrating deep into the Chinle Formation. The wealth of topographical forms results from the differing ability of the materials to resist, sandstone, limestone, and lava eroding less rapidly than clay and slate. These harder strata form the visible elements of the Painted Desert.

Painted Desert

The name Painted Desert is found in various parts of North American deserts, although the quasi-official one is situated in the north of the Petrified Forest National Park. Visitors often combine the two in one trip to the northeast bank of the Little Colorado, which joins the Colorado immediately to the east of the Grand Canyon National Monument. This is an extremely dry, barren stretch of country boasting neither vegetation nor any kind of attractive feature. No one would come here voluntarily, were it not for the predominantly horizontal rock strata with their peculiar and amazing array of colors—red, violet, light yellow, white, blue. In a word, nature here presents a show of color such as even the wildest human imagination would hardly be capable of inventing. Although red predominates, all kinds of different tones are caused by the iron oxides which have percolated through the sandstone over millions of years (49, 50, 51).

Two hundred million years ago, Arizona was a tropical region very near the Equator. According to the continental shift theory, today's large land bodies once lay close together, forming a supercontinent called Pangaea. When this gigantic land mass disintegrated the different blocks drifted apart, the one incorporating what was destined to be Arizona moving northwest and finally taking up its present position along with the rest of the North American continent. Mesozoic Arizona was a flat, low-lying area crossed by rivers large and small which imprinted their meanderings onto the landscape and washed mud and sand along to form a multitude of strata. In the course of millions of years these sediments built up a layer over 3,000 feet thick, which

47 Canyon de Chelly National Monument/Arizona

to collect and sell these magnificent stones, it was decided that conservation measures were called for. Restrictions were imposed on use of the most important parts of the petrified forest in 1906, and the 220 square miles which now make up Petrified Forest National Park acquired legal status in 1970. In order to preserve the precious formations by discouraging theft, the authorities permit the sale of small samples which come from other regions and are sold by licensed dealers.

In 1985 the petrified skeleton of a plateosaurus was discovered near Chinde Point in the northern part of the park. This herbivorous animal the size of an Alsatian dog probably lived some two hundred twenty-five million years ago and is regarded as the ancestor of the more recent giant brontosaurus. The find caused a great sensation and the animal was immediately given the nickname "Gertie." American experts consider it to be the oldest dinosaur yet discovered.

52

53

51 Painted Desert / Arizona

Petrified Forest

This arid plateau was once fertile. Two hundred twenty-five million years ago, massive trees grew here: Arancaria xylon, Woodworthia, and Schilderia. Huge trunks swept away by later flooding were eventually covered with mud and sand roughly two hundred million years ago. Most important, air was excluded, and the resulting absence of oxygen prevented the trees from decomposing in the normal way. Groundwater containing silicon penetrated into the trunks and the woody tissue was gradually replaced by silicon residues. This process continued at a slow pace until finally, after many thousands if not millions of years, the trees were petrified.

The whole region was lifted up about sixty-five million years ago and once again covered with sediments. Later, wind and water freed the trunks from the layers of material protecting them. Thus the petrified trees, together with plants and animals which had suffered the same fate, eventually came to light. Particularly striking is the way in which the gigantic trunks have broken up, the smooth breaks making them look as though they have been sawn into pieces (54–56).

The oldest settlements date back to the pre-Christian era. Indians inhabited the region from 1100 to 1200 and from 1300 to 1400 A.D., but they too abandoned their stone dwellings (now known as the Puerco Ruins). The sixteenth century saw the arrival of the Spaniards, who introduced their own way of life, and many of today's place names date from that period. The first Americans made their appearance during the eigthteenth century and soon realized that pieces of petrified trees would make good ornaments because of their coloring. When it became fashionable

White Sands

Two roads lead northwards from El Paso (Texas), which lies on the border with Mexico. The main route follows the Rio Grande to Albuquerque and Santa Fe, capital of New Mexico, while a secondary one runs almost parallel to it through the more or less arid Tularosa Valley bounded on the east by the Sacramento Mountains and on the west by the San Andres Mountains. On a level with Alamogordo is the White Sands National Monument, a National Park covering 370 square miles and lying only a little to the west of the main road.

White Sands Dunes form the southern part of an extensive desert area long used by the United States Government as a military and technical training and proving ground. As a tourist attraction, the dunes were declared a National Monument in 1933. The area achieved fame in World War II, when the desert zones adjoining it to the north came into use as a military training ground. Today, White Sands is used for space trials in connection with the space shuttle.

A most attractive feature of the dunes—to which the public has access—is a well-made sixteen-mile circuit of road consisting partly of pure gypsum and running through a strange, white landscape. The substances of which the dunes are composed—calcium sulphate, gypsum dust, and gypsum grains of varying sizes—come from gypsum strata in the two mountain ranges mentioned earlier. Geologists have pinpointed two sediments as being particularly rich in calcium sulphate: Yeso and San Andres. The dunes came into being over the last 25,000 years. The prevailing southwesterly winds are constantly shifting them towards the northeast. Normally blowing at

5 miles per hour, the wind can reach speeds of as much as 45 mph when sandstorms get up. The dynamics of this process have their origin in Lake Lucero, a small expanse of water in a flat hollow. Covering approximately one-and-a-half square miles, the lake forms after the summer rains, but soon dries out again.

The most energetic of the dunes advance about 20 feet a year and the largest reach a height of 36 feet. Despite the altitude of 3,600 feet above sea level, summertime brings stifling heat. Under those conditions, visitors find it a relief to climb to the crest of a dune to be refreshed by the steady southwest wind. Many enjoy sliding down from the tops of the dunes.

The vegetation is far from attractive. Practically the only plants to flourish here are of the desert variety: the salt bush and the iodine bush. Although it may seem surprising to find cottonwood growing in the hollows, this is explained by the presence of groundwater only a few feet beneath the surface. The vegetation plays a crucial role—as in all dune regions, the stability of the shifting sands depends upon the survival of small plants. It is well worth the visitor's while, therefore, to take a closer look at these living organisms in their struggle for existence. With an annual rainfall of about 10 inches. White Sands is to all intents in the clutches of a desert climate. The plants' fight for survival suggests some interesting lines of thought.

Gypsum is an eroded limestone containing few visible color constituents and consequently appearing in a brilliant, warm white. Both the mountain ranges referred to incorporate gypsum

strata which were brought to the surface by tectonic movements (elevation, folding, massif formation), eroded by weathering, and carried to the lowest-lying part of the Tularosa Basin.

Anyone who walks alone through the dunes of White Sands takes poignant memories away with him. Lowered to the immediate surroundings, the eye becomes engrossed with the fine patterns wrought on the surface by the wind. A system of folds large and small—deceptively similar yet never identical—seems fixed into the sand, though in reality in almost constant motion. Raised to the dunes around, our gaze rests with pleasure on their infinitely gentle forms. Finally, as we lift our eyes to the great vista, we find the dune landscape inducing a sensation of immeasurable space and timelessness; one could easily imagine oneself to be looking at an Arctic or Antarctic snowcape. Certainly, no one who visits this region can escape the sense of isolation.

This, indeed, is probably the keenest impression inspired by the National Monuments described in this book. At a time when huge numbers of people live in ever bigger cities amidst growing fears of overpopulation, space and emptiness devoid of human habitation hold an unconscious attraction. Visitors are thrilled not only by the magnificent colors and forms, but equally by the exhilarating sensation of solitude. And it may be, that quiet contemplation of these photographs will reconcile us somewhat to the bustle of everyday life.

Sigmund Widmer

63 White Sands National Monument/New Mexico

Travel Notes

In 1953 I set out with Hans-Ulrich Meier on my first trip to the USA. During that five-month assignment for the monthly magazine "Du" we motored through 30 states, covering a total of 17,000 miles. After more than three decades the fascination of this land of infinite surprises still remains, particularly in the southwest and west where a series of spectacular panoramas reveals a slice of the earth's history. Thirty years on, the pent-up urge to return had grown so strong that I decided to revisit some of the regions we had passed through on that first journey. Although much had undoubtedly changed on the tourist front, this renewed encounter left an equally vivid impression on me and I found myself toying increasingly with the idea of producing a book based on my collection of photographs. I set off in the autumn of 1983 accompanied by my friend Jack Kunz.

As the Arizona newspapers reported at the time, it was the "worst autumn of the century." The Gila River had swept away a section of Interstate Highway 10 not far from Phoenix, flooding large areas. This unusual scenario fitted in very well with my plans for the photo album. My recollection of Monument Valley thirty years earlier, for example, was of an arid desert covered with an ankle-deep layer of red dust under a cloudless sky. This time, it was only thanks to our four-wheel drive Subaru that we got permission to drive into the monument valley and managed to get across chocolate-colored torrents under a sky heavy with cloud. Near the Totem Pole we even came upon a waterfall tinged blood-red by the earth (33).

As I wanted to include some attractive bird's-eye views in the book, I flew to Arizona once again in August 1984 to make various preparations: not only was it necessary to arrange for a helicopter to be available to us, but it also had to be equipped to carry my remote-controlled rotating camera which had been specially designed for taking panoramic photographs.

Two months later, then, I set out for the southwest of the United States for the fourth time, on this occasion with my son Fredy. That part of the world wasn't in fact entirely new to Fredy either: an experienced glider pilot, he had competed in the world championships at Hobbs, New Mexico, only a year before. As it turned out, his flying skills were to be of no little help to us. The notes Fredy made on the journey recall that unforgettable adventure in the air, giving an idea of the critical situations which can put such undertakings at serious risk: "We've been flying for several hours on our second day. The helicopter needs refuelling as soon as possible, which means Airport Grand Canyon. I'm sitting between Dudley—the pilot—and Pa. Dudley's trying to radio the Tower... No reply! He swears and bangs the radio set with his first. Has it broken down? Then I notice from the ICAO flight map that he's using the wrong frequency. I correct it and we get through to the Tower. 'Very good, navigator,' laughs Dudley. After refuelling we fly down the Canyon to shoot some more panoramas. But the weather begins to worsen rapidly, so Pa suggests we fly straight back to base. We pass over the densely wooded Kaibab Plateau and just then I smell smoke. In seconds the cabin fills with an acrid cloud that gets thicker and thicker. Dudley has to land in a hurry on a small area of rock next to a jagged arm of Marble Canyon—with the panoramic camera still slung underneath on a 15-foot cable ready for shooting... We get out quickly, relieved to feel solid ground under our feet again. Taking a closer look, we can see the helicopter has a huge leak from a damaged oil pipe... Now we know the reason for the smoke: oil was pouring out over the hot engine. After considering briefly what a fire on board would have meant, we quickly come back to reality: the helicopter will obviously have to stay where it is. It's almost five o'clock in the evening and we're in an uninhabited region of rocky desert without a road in sight anywhere. We stow the camera and other equipment away in the cabin and set off eastwards. Time is running short: very soon it's dark and the nights here get uncomfortably cold. Again and again we have to clamber through small side canyons, some of them pretty steep. At last, shortly after dark, we reach a road where a helpful motorist finally gives us a lift."

By the summer of 1987, work on the plan for the book and the artwork aspect had already been completed. Even the technical preparations for its printing had reached an advanced stage. Nevertheless, I had to go back a fifth time to that world of primeval rock structures because two or three of the photographs kept on nagging me: I just couldn't help feeling they needed redoing from the point of view of the book's structure as well as its overall presentation.

It came home to me forcibly yet again in the course of this last journey that the ultimate reality of this unique and simply unforgettable world of physical forms lies beyond the power of the human imagination, exceeds normal optical dimensions and cannot in fact be adequately captured by any camera. You need to have seen it, to have actually stood in the midst of it: no image can ever hope to reproduce the overwhelming mightiness of these primordial landscapes.

In 1984, on my third journey to the southwest of the United States in the course of my work preparing this collection of photographs, I was accompanied by my wife. It was to be our last journey together and she has not been here to witness the making, printing, and publication of the present volume. This book is dedicated to the memory of my beloved Bruna with special affection and gratitude.

Emil Schulthess

Acknowledgment

I am most grateful to Dr. Sigmund Widmer, former Mayor of Zurich, for his substantial contribution to this book. My thanks also go to Dr. Hans F. Vögeli, who was particularly helpful in the book's publication. As on former occasions, my friend Bruno Mariacher looked after the publishing side. Valuable assistance also came from the following persons and institutions:

George J. Berklacy, National Park Service, Washington D.C.; Isadore Beckman, CBS New York; Howard Chapnick, Black Star New York; Bert Diener, Swissair Zürich-Kloten; Prof. Dr. Emil Egli, Zürich; Larry Giannesetti, CBS New York; Fritz Girardin, Zürich; Gravor SA, Biel; Chris Gross, Streag AG, Safenwil; Dudley Hale, Page/Arizona; Verena Horvath, Zürich; Leo Kalmus, Biel; Jack Kunz, Pfaffhausen; Goro Kuramochi, G.I.P. Tokyo; Dr. André Lambert, Zürich;
Cliff Langness, Lake Powell Air Service, Page/Arizona; Hans-Ulrich Meier, Paris; Willy Messerli, Biel; Will Prater, Oakland/California; Lee Reichenthal, CBS New York; Bruno Murbach, Biel; Ole Risom, New York; Kurt Schaad, Zürich; Buchbinderei Schumacher AG, Bern/Schmitten; Seitz Phototechnik, Lustdorf; Philip M. Smith, National Academy of Sciences, Washington D.C.; Alois Stutz, Bremgarten; Weber Farbendruck AG, Biel; Mike Whelan, Pennsauken/New Jersey.

E.S.